The Little Giant

By

Pauline Francis

First published in 2001
by Anglia Young Books
Anglia Young Books is an imprint of
MILL Publishing
PO Box 55
4 Balloo Avenue
Bangor
Co. Down BT19 7PJ

© 2001 Pauline Francis

All rights reserved. No part of this publication
may be reproduced, stored in a retrieval system,
or transmitted in any form or by any means,
electronic, mechanical, photocopying, recording
or otherwise without the written permission
of the Publisher.

The moral right of the author has been asserted.

Illustrations by Robin Lawrie

British Library Cataloguing-in-Publication Data

A catalogue record for this book is available
from the British Library

ISBN 1 871173 70 1

Printed in Great Britain by
Ashford Colour Press, Gosport, Hampshire

The Little Giant

AUTHOR'S NOTE

Between 1760 and 1860, during the reigns of King William IV and Queen Victoria, there were enormous changes in England. We now call this time the Industrial Revolution. Machines, turned by water power, were invented. Many factories were built in the hills near fast running water. Then steam changed the world for ever. James Watt built a steam engine in 1769 and within a few years, steam was used instead of water power. This meant that factories could be built in towns and cities. People left the countryside to work in them.

There was a group of well-known engineers who were designing and building bridges, tunnels, railways and machines – men such as Thomas Telford, George Stephenson and Isambard Kingdom Brunel. They were all great engineers, but Isambard had an extra and very important quality: he thought on a large scale. Thus his story is one of great success and great failure.

Many books have been written about Isambard Kingdom Brunel. Some praise him because his designs were brilliant and new. Others criticize him for being too interested in fame and fortune. Isambard kept a diary from about the age of fourteen. He also wrote many letters to his friends and family when he was away from them. More importantly, his son, Isambard, wrote about his famous father in 1870 – *The Life of Isambard Kingdom Brunel, Civil Engineer.'* Later, Celia Brunel

Noble, his daughter-in-law, also wrote a book called *'The Brunels, Father and Son.'* Some of this material has been used in this book.

Chapter One
The Second Brick

On 9 April, 1806, a baby boy was born in Britain Street, Portsmouth, a busy port on the south coast of England. The baby's father, a Frenchman called Marc Isambard Brunel, was overjoyed. Although he and his wife, Sophia Kingdom, already had two daughters, he wanted a son desperately. Marc Isambard Brunel was an engineer – he designed tunnels, bridges and machines – and in the nineteenth century, girls could not become engineers. He wanted a son who would become an engineer like him.

Marc Brunel planned his son's future from the day Isambard was born. 'I want you to become an engineer,' he told him. 'So *I* shall teach you some maths *before* you go to school.' Isambard was very quick to understand shapes. When he was only four years old, he could draw a perfect circle.

Isambard also loved drawing and painting. He enjoyed putting on plays with his sisters, but his father did not encourage these hobbies. He wanted Isambard to spend his spare time learning all he could about engineering. 'Engineers are very important,' he told his son, 'because there are great changes taking place in this country.' He smiled fondly at his young son. '*You* will be part of these great changes.'

Isambard watched his father's work closely. One day, he learned a very important lesson. He must use his eyes as well as his brains. That day, Mr. Brunel came home from the Portsmouth shipyard where he was working. He was excited. He looked as if he was planning something.

'I came across some old wood from one of the ships today,' Mr. Brunel said. 'It was full of worm-holes. I took my magnifying glass and looked inside one of the holes. I watched a worm for a long time. It has given me a new idea.'

That same day, Isambard watched his father start to design a new machine. It was called a tunnelling shield. It was made of metal, with a cutting edge. Men would stand behind it, push the earth forward with it, and line the tunnel behind with bricks so that it wouldn't collapse.

The movement of the shield was a perfect copy of the worm's movements through the wood.

'But what are you going to use it for?' Isambard asked his father. 'I'm going to build a tunnel under the River Thames,' his father replied. 'Many have tried and failed. I shall succeed.'

Isambard listened in great excitement. 'London Bridge is the only bridge across the River Thames,' his father explained. 'People have to use ferries, and they are slow and dangerous. This tunnel will make me famous.'

From then on, Marc Isambard Brunel talked of little else. It became an obsession with him. And he wanted his son to be ready to help him. But this was all in the future. It would take some years to build the tunnelling shield, and raise some money to start the tunnel. And during that time, the young Isambard had to study engineering!

Meanwhile, the family moved to Chelsea, which was then a small village close to London. It was perfect for the noisy and energetic Isambard. The River Thames flowed past the bottom of the garden. Isambard learned to swim and to row a small boat. However, the river water was very dirty and Isambard was often ill from swallowing it.

When Isambard was nine years old, he was sent to school in Hove, a town on the south coast of England. By then, his letters show that already he thought like an engineer. 'I have been making half a dozen boats lately,' he wrote to his parents, 'till I've worn my hands to pieces.' He understood building design because he was so good at maths. One day, a new building was begun opposite Isambard's school. He watched the building work for a few days, then said to his friends, 'It will fall down. I'll take bets on it!' During the night, a loud noise woke everybody up. The building had crashed to the ground!

When he was fourteen years old,

Isambard went to study in France. His father thought he would have a better education there, and he wanted him to learn French. Isambard became a pupil at a famous school in Paris. He studied maths and science. At the same time, he worked with a man who made scientific instruments.

At the same time, Marc Isambard Brunel was trying to make a lot of money to build the tunnel. He had a really good idea – again! This time, he *would* make a fortune from it! War had broken out between England and France. 'What do our soldiers need in a hurry?' Mr. Brunel asked himself. 'Boots!' He invented a machine to make thousands of boots. But the war ended suddenly. There were eighty thousand boots left over. The British government refused to buy them. Marc Brunel was sent to prison for three months because he owed so much money, and was set free only with the help of a friend. It was a very worrying time for Isambard. But it made him even more determined to be more famous and richer than his father.

Isambard came back to England when he was seventeen. By this time, Marc Brunel had a small office in London. He was looking forward to working at last with his clever son. He could see that Isambard had all the right qualities to be a very good engineer. Isambard had more than a good brain and a good education – he had enthusiasm and never gave up, even if things went wrong. The family still didn't have much money, but they had enough. And now Marc Isambard Brunel, with the help of his son, was close to achieving his great ambition – the Thames Tunnel.

Isambard began to keep a diary. He was very happy to be back with his family and to be living in London. He soon made a lot of friends because he was such good fun. He liked sport. He and a friend had a small rowing boat. They spent hours rowing up and down on the Thames. And as he rowed, Isambard thought, 'Soon people will be able to walk *under* this river through *our* tunnel.'

In March, 1825, when Isambard was nineteen years old, he stood next to his father at a place called Cow Court in Rotherhithe, by the River Thames. Church bells rang out, flags fluttered, bands played and famous visitors stood to watch. Marc Isambard Brunel placed the first brick at the entrance to the

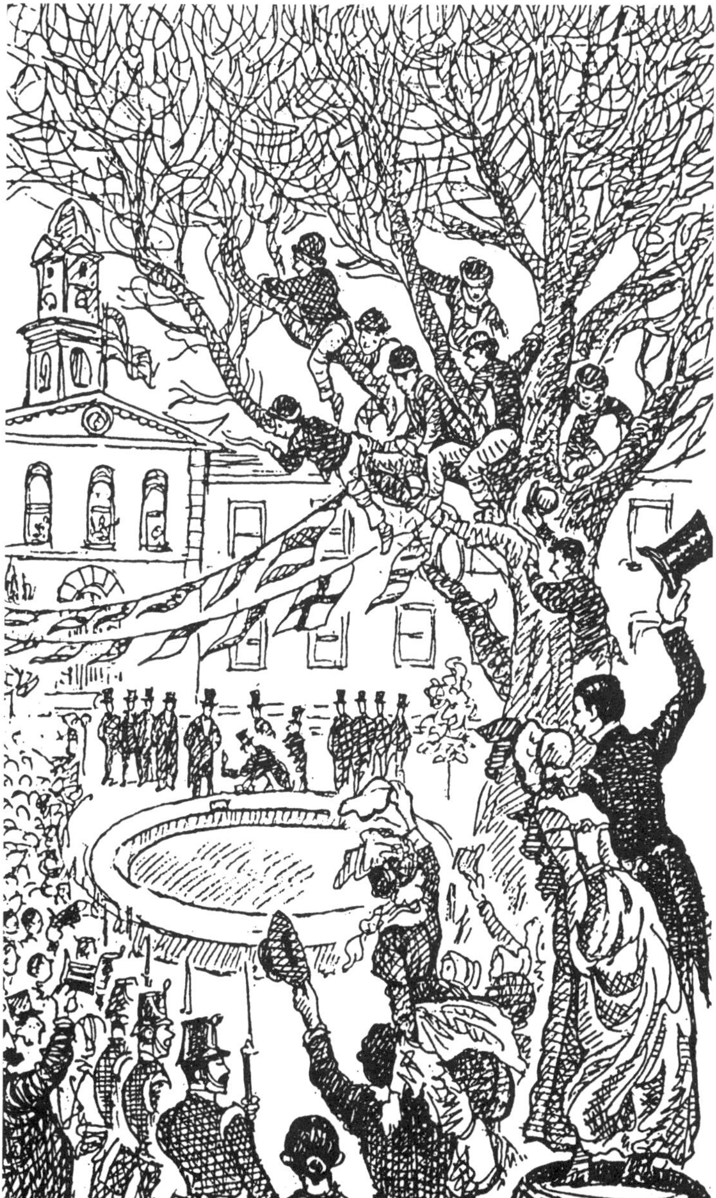

Thames Tunnel. Then Isambard stepped forward proudly and laid the second brick.

That brick marked the beginning of Isambard Kingdom Brunel's engineering career.

Chapter Two
Danger Underground

Soon after the work on the tunnel began, Isambard's father became ill. So, at the age of twenty, Isambard was in charge of a project which was the talk of Europe. He was confident about the work. But one thing worried Isambard. He was now in charge of the men who did the tunnelling. They were miners – big and strong with powerful muscles from digging out coal underground. They joked and swore and sometimes drank a lot – and they expected men to be tough. Isambard was only five feet tall. He never did grow any taller, although he hoped he would. 'What if the men laugh at me?' he thought. 'What if they refuse to obey my orders? I *must* find a way of looking older and taller.'

Isambard started to wear a very tall top hat called a stovepipe hat. And he started to smoke cigars. In a famous photograph of Isambard, taken many years later, you can see a leather strap across his waistcoat. This was to hold the bag of spare cigars that he always carried.

Did Isambard really need his hat and his cigars? No! He had a good sense of humour and he was good at his job. And, most important of all, he was not afraid to get his hands dirty. Sometimes he worked with the men on the tunnelling shield for thirty-six hours without stopping. His men always respected him.

Isambard was a very flamboyant young man. This meant that he chose to behave in a way that made people notice him. Perhaps it was because he was small! But nobody minded, because he was always such good fun. When it was time to celebrate his twenty-first birthday, Isambard told his parents, 'I shall have my birthday party in the tunnel.' And he did! After that, people began to visit the tunnel for a day out. It was a good way of raising money for the work. But Isambard was worried. Water from the River Thames was rising in the tunnel.

One day, Isambard was working in the tunnel with a hundred and sixty men. There was an enormous roar above their heads and water burst into the tunnel. Isambard rescued many men because he was such a good swimmer. Luckily, nobody was killed that day. Many other floods happened after that. But Isambard used it as a way of making money. Sightseers came in boats to see the floods for themselves.

Sometimes, Isambard enjoyed frightening his visitors. Once, when he was in a boat with them, he stood up to light the top of the tunnel with a candle. He fell into the water because he fooled around too much. His terrified visitors were plunged into darkness. Isambard swam to the surface and climbed back onto the boat.

'He is a foolish young man,' some people said, 'and he takes too many risks.' But other people said, 'He is only trying to raise money to finish the tunnel.' A newspaper made a joke about the tunnel by calling it 'The Great Bore.' But most people admired Isambard's courage and determination.

A few months after the floods, when the tunnel was dry again, Isambard arranged an important dinner for fifty famous guests – and all his workmen. The brick arches of the tunnel were hung with crimson cloths and lit with a candelabra using a new gas. A band of guardsmen played music all evening. This was Isambard's way of showing the public that the Thames Tunnel was safe.

But eight months later, there was a very serious flood. Isambard was working on the shield at six o'clock in the morning of 12 January, 1828. The watchman came running into the office shouting, 'The tunnel's full. The tunnel's full.' Isambard's assistant ran from the office to the visitors' staircase. He smashed open the locked door and hurried down the steps. At the bottom, he found the unconscious body of Isambard. In a few seconds, the water would rush back from the tunnel and take Isambard with it. There wasn't much time. Horrified, the man dragged Isambard slowly up the steps. He

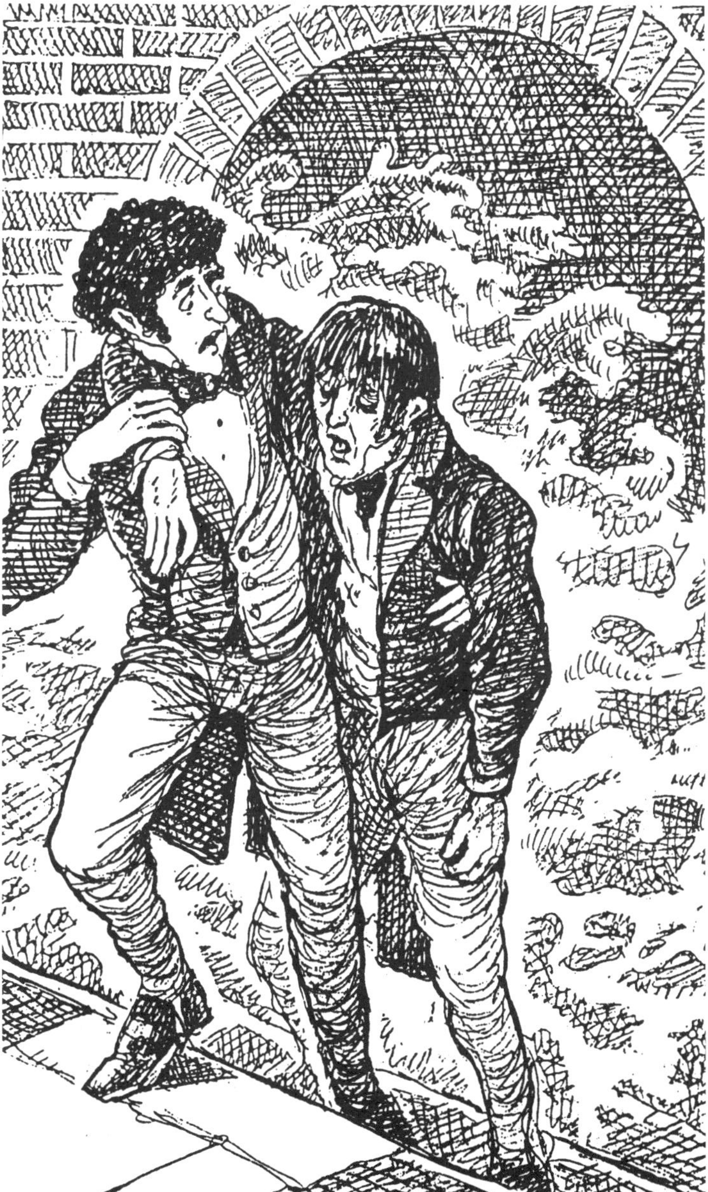

had narrowly escaped death, thanks to his assistant. This was to be the first of many times. Isambard wrote in his diary: '...I never expected we should get out...'

There was no more money to finish the tunnel. Marc Brunel was ill and his son was injured. Work stopped. Isambard did not miss a chance. He ordered an enormous mirror to be fixed at the tunnel entrance so that people could pay to see the reflection of his great work.

However, it was this accident in the tunnel that led Isambard Kingdom Brunel to design one of the most famous bridges in Britain today.

Chapter Three
The Hanging Bridge

Isambard was sent to Clifton to get better. This was a small town outside Bristol, a large port in the west of England. There, he had plenty of time to think about what he wanted from life.

'I've enjoyed working with my father,' he told his friends. 'He has taught me a lot. But now I want to be independent. I have my own ideas about engineering.' Isambard also wanted to be famous, but he was probably too modest to say so then!

Clifton was very beautiful. It stood on the banks of a deep gorge. The River Avon ran through the gorge and brought ships up to Bristol. Isambard spent most of his time drawing the sailing boats below him, or the views on the other side of the gorge.

One day, Isambard read about a competition in the local newspaper. The rich people of Clifton wanted a bridge built across the River Avon and they asked engineers to send in a design. It would be a difficult job. The gorge was too deep for pillars to rise from the river bed. The bridge would have to be hung right across the gorge.

'This is my chance,' thought Isambard. 'If I win the competition, I could be the most famous engineer in Britain.'

As soon as he could, Isambard travelled by horse and coach to North Wales to see the Menai Bridge. A man called Thomas Telford had designed and built it four years before. It was the first suspension, or hanging, bridge in the world – and it is still used today.

Isambard entered his design in the competition. One of the judges was Thomas Telford. He didn't like any of the designs! He thought they were all very dangerous.

Isambard was so disappointed and angry that he smoked one cigar after another!

A second competition was held soon afterwards. Isambard entered more designs, and this time, he won. A few months later, in June 1831, work on the bridge began. Once again, Isambard Kingdom Brunel was at the centre of a huge crowd. The first stones were dug from the side of the gorge. Important people stood round them in a circle. As Isambard stepped forward to pick up a stone, cannon guns boomed across the Avon Gorge. Down in the gorge, guardsmen played the National Anthem. People said at the time that Isambard Kingdom Brunel would build 'the ornament of Bristol and the wonder of the age.' These words were true, but sadly, not in his lifetime.

Isambard was excited by his new project. But unfortunately, work stopped and started on the Clifton Suspension Bridge for many years. There was nothing wrong with the design of the bridge. Isambard's first great engineering work suffered from a very common problem – lack of money. And there was another serious problem – street riots in Bristol. Thousands of men were unhappy

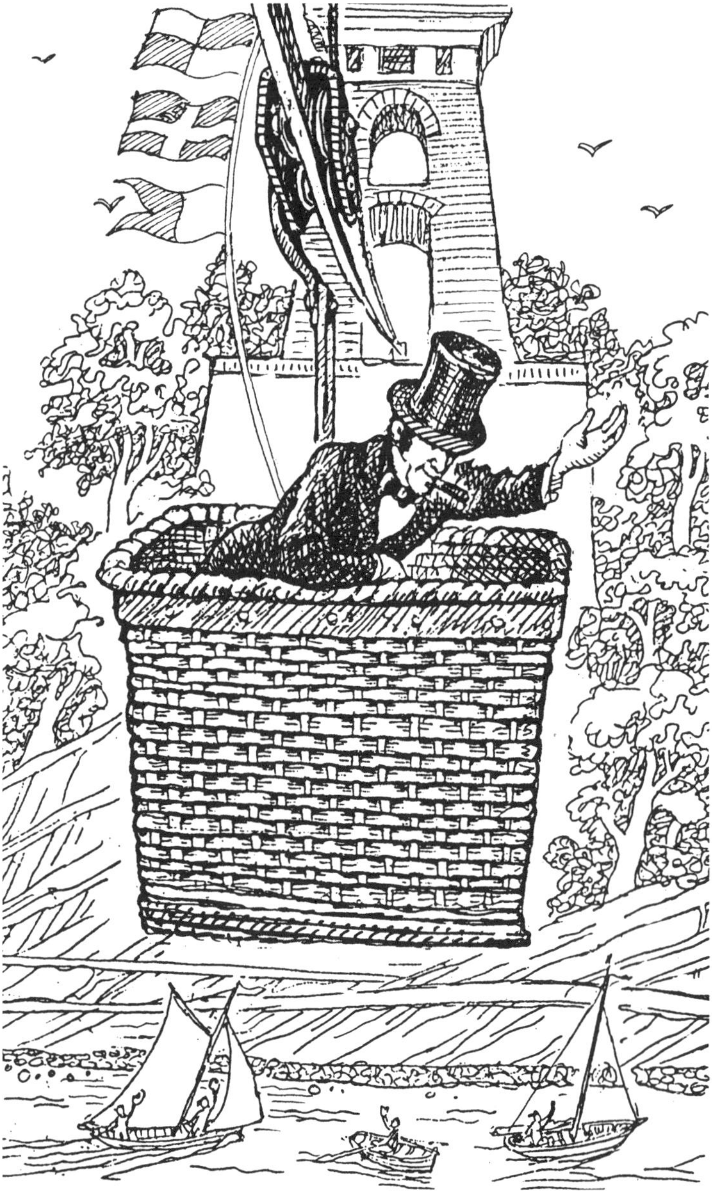

because they weren't allowed to vote. Only a few months after the army band had played at the opening of the bridge, they were trying to keep order in the city streets.

Work *did* begin again soon after the riots ended. A few years later, the towers of the bridge, which would hold the chains, were completed. Then the money ran out again. It was very frustrating for Isambard. But the twin towers were put to good use. An iron bar, one thousand feet long, ran from one to the other. A basket hung from it. It was pulled across the gorge by ropes. Isambard himself travelled across to make sure it was safe. The bar and basket were used to raise some money, and provided a crossing for anyone brave enough to try it!

Nobody blamed Isambard. People knew that he was a great engineer. He had provided a brilliant design for the bridge. It wasn't *his* job to raise the money. The Clifton Suspension Bridge was finished in December,1864, five years after Isambard's death. His friends finished it in his memory. It is sad to think that Isambard Kingdom Brunel never saw it. He is best known today for this bridge, although it wasn't all his own work.

Luckily for Isambard, the rich businessmen of Bristol became very worried about something that had happened in the north of England. It was something new and exciting for the people who lived there – a railway line had been built between the port of Liverpool and the city of Manchester.

Until then, there were no railways in Britain. People travelled in coaches pulled by horses. They were uncomfortable and slow. There were no tunnels. The muddy, rough roads had to go round steep hills making the journey dangerous. It was difficult to carry coal to the new factories. Coal was needed to make steam to turn the machines. Sometimes, the coal was carried on canals. Sometimes, it was carried in wagons pulled by horses, along metal tracks called railroads. Someone tried out a steam engine in place of the horse. That was how the railway began.

The Manchester-Liverpool Railway carried passengers as well as coal and other goods from the factories to the steamships in Liverpool. Bristol was a port like Liverpool. Now people were worried. There was no railway from Bristol to London. What if ships sailed to Liverpool instead of Bristol? Some businessmen in Bristol set up the Great Western Railway Company. And they asked Isambard to become their Chief Engineer.

At the age of twenty-seven, Isambard Kingdom Brunel became one of the most important, and well-paid, engineers in Britain.

Chapter Four
God's Great Railway

'This railway will make me very famous,' Isambard thought, 'but please God there will be enough money this time to finish the job.'

    Isambard joined the company in March, 1833. Immediately, he had to carry out a survey of all the land between London and Bristol by May – a distance of 118 miles. He rode many miles every day, sometimes as much as forty. He wrote in his diary: 'Just as I got in sight of Windsor Castle, my horse came down – cut his knees and forehead dreadfully – I just scratched my knee.'

Then he had to design the whole railway and the huge steam engines that would pull the trains. Isambard knew he would have to work night and day. So he designed a special carriage for his journeys, pulled by four horses. It contained his office, a bed - and enormous boxes of cigars! Isambard said to an assistant: 'It is harder work than I like. I am rarely much under twenty hours a day at it.'

Fortunately, Isambard already had very strong ideas about the sort of railway he wanted to build. He had already travelled on Stephenson's railway between Liverpool and Manchester. On the train, he had written in his diary, in very wobbly handwriting: 'I record this specimen of the shaking of the Manchester railway. The time is not far off when we shall be able to take our coffee and write while going along noiselessly and smoothly at 45 m.p.h. – let me try.'

Isambard made a very bold decision. 'I am going to use a wider track than Stephenson did,' he told the men in the company. 'The trains will not sway around so much, and they will be able to carry more passengers.' Isambard boasted that everyone would use his wide track in the future – but this did not happen.

To Isambard's surprise, the people in Parliament didn't like his plans for the railway. They were mainly people who had never seen a railway. 'It will spoil my land,' one man said. 'It will make the countryside noisy and dirty,' said another. One important man even complained that the new railroads 'would encourage the lower classes to move about.'

So Isambard started all over again! After two years, he sent in another plan. He even went to Parliament for eleven days to answer questions about the railway. One man was very rude to him. But Isambard was polite. He smiled all the time and came up with a good answer to every question. When it was all over, and the plan was accepted, a friend asked Isambard: 'How did you stay so calm when faced with such a rude man. Isambard answered: 'Because he could not possibly know as much about engineering as I.'

It is difficult for us today, with all our digging machines, to imagine what it was like then to build such a railway. The men only had shovels and pick-axes to dig with, and wheelbarrows to take away the earth. However, there were plenty of workmen, or 'navvies.' Hundreds of men came from Ireland to work on the railway because there was little work in their own country.

Building began in 1835. The railway was finished in sections. There were huge problems to be solved every day. Some people were quick to laugh at Isambard when things went wrong. 'George Stephenson is the only man who knows how to build railways,' they sneered. At the end of 1837, Isambard wrote to a friend: 'If ever I go mad, I shall have the ghost of the opening of the railway walking before me.'

One section of the railway was really dangerous. This was the line between the towns of Chippenham and Bath. A huge tunnel was needed. It was called the Box Tunnel. It was 2 miles long, the longest tunnel at that time. Every week for two and a half years, this tunnel used up a tonne of candles and a tonne of gunpowder. It used thirty million bricks. And it used up men. Out of four thousand workers, one hundred died.

When the two tunnels met in the middle, they were only two centimetres out. Isambard was so pleased with the man in charge of the workers that he took a ring from his finger and gave it to him. This was the secret of Isambard's success with people. He knew how to manage his men. He asked for loyalty. He was loyal to them. The story of the ring was remembered long after the number of the dead men had been forgotten.

This tunnel is said to be the finest in England, and is still used today. There is a story that says that the sun shines through the Box Tunnel on Isambard's birthday. Modern scientists have checked this, by measuring the angle of the sun's rays on that day. They say it is *just* possible.

The Great Western Railway was finished quickly. On the 30 June, 1841, the first train left Bristol for Paddington Station in London. The 150 mile journey now took five and a half hours. Until then, people had to use a stage coach which took twenty hours, and was very uncomfortable.

A year later, Isambard travelled with Queen Victoria on this railway. The young Queen, who had been on the throne for just five years, was the first ruler ever to travel by train. She travelled in a beautiful Royal Saloon

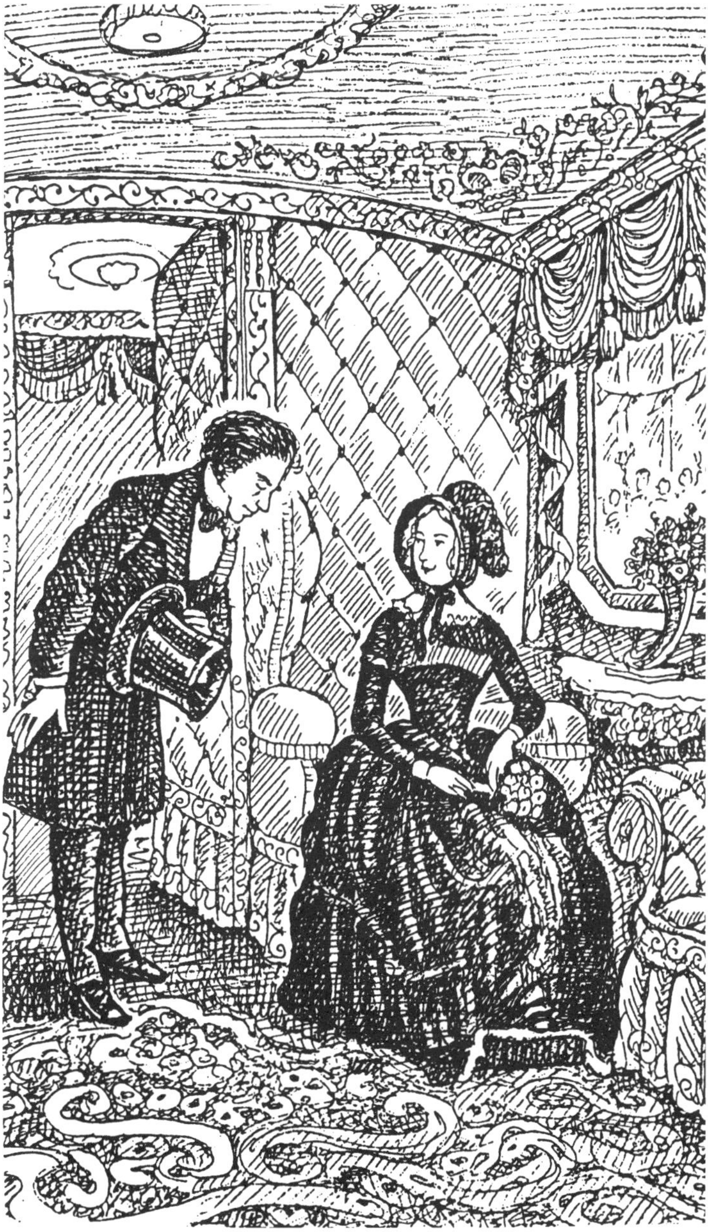

carriage from Swindon (near Windsor Castle) to Paddington Station in London. She later wrote to her uncle: 'We arrived yesterday morning, having come by the railroad from Windsor, in half an hour, free from dust and crowd and heat, and I am quite charmed with it.'

Isambard must have felt very proud. Once the Queen had used his railway, he knew that everybody would. The passengers loved it and called it 'God's Wonderful Railway.' And Isambard's workers called him 'The Little Giant,' a nickname that stayed with him for the rest of his life.

The Great Western Railway was very important. It was four times longer than the Liverpool-Manchester Railway. Everybody wanted more railways when they saw how good it was. By 1850, there were almost four thousand miles of railway lines linking all main cities and sea ports. The Great Western Railway itself expanded to reach the south coast of England, most of Devon and Cornwall, South Wales and Birmingham and the Midlands.

As well as carrying goods from the factories to the sea ports, the railways carried newspapers and post quickly to all towns and cities. It is difficult to believe now, but until then, the time on the clock was slightly different all over England. But the railways had to use a timetable. For the first time, the same clock time had to be used everywhere – we call this Greenwich Mean Time.

This enormous job proved that Isambard Kingdom Brunel was a brilliant engineer who kept an eye on all the details - the track layout, the track, the trains, the bridges, the tunnels, the railway stations and even the lamp posts for them! Yet in the midst of all this activity, Isambard found time to design a luxury hotel at Paddington Station *and* a steamship to take passengers from Bristol to New York. He showed the enormous vision which made him great.

Chapter Five
The family man

Mary Brunel

The day after Christmas 1835, four months after the start of the Great Western Railway, Isambard found time to write in his diary again. He was very happy with life, and he even boasted a little. He made a list of all his work in the past year – and added something at the end! He wrote:

> *'Clifton Bridge - my first child, my darling, is actually going on -*
> *Sunderland Docks too going well -*

Bristol Docks
Suspension Bridge across the Thames -
Mrs. B - this time 12 months I shall be a
married man.

'Mrs. B' (Mrs. Brunel) shows us that Isambard was thinking of getting married. True to his plan, he married the following summer. Isambard seemed to plan his marriage as he planned the rest of his life – with careful efficiency. His wife was called Mary Horsley. She was a very grand lady, from a rich family. She was beautiful and elegant; but she did not share her husband's sense of humour.

Isambard was proud of Mary because she made their home look beautiful. She also gave parties for famous people. Although Isambard was already an important man, Mary brought him into contact with other people who could help him. Her brother John, an artist, became a close friend and painted Isambard's portrait.

Isambard and Mary had a fine house in London. Whenever Mary went for a walk in the park, she ordered her carriage to follow slowly behind in case she became tired.

Three children were born. Isambard's

first son, born in 1838, was named after him and was always known as Isambard the Third. He wasn't a very strong boy and didn't want to become an engineer. Isambard was disappointed. However, Isambard the Third had one claim to fame. He was the first person to cross the River Thames *under* the water! The Thames Tunnel was finished in 1843, when Isambard the Third was three years old. As the two ends of the tunnel met, he was passed through the tunnel. In fact, fifty thousand people walked through the tunnel that day, including Queen Victoria. The Thames Tunnel was as important as the Channel Tunnel is today, and it is still used by the London Underground railway.

Isambard's second son, Henry Marc, was born in 1842. He became an engineer, although he wasn't as famous as his father, and helped to design Tower Bridge in London. Mary was born four years after Henry.

Of course, Isambard spent a great deal of time away from home or in his office on the ground floor of their house. But he always tried to say goodnight to his children in the nursery.

Isambard liked to play tricks on his

children. His favourite trick used a coin. 'Watch me swallow this coin!' he told his excited children. He put the coin into his mouth and pretended to swallow it. Then he put his hand up to his ear. 'Now, what have I got here?' And he took the coin from his ear. His children loved this trick and asked him to do it over and over again.

Once when Henry was a baby, Isambard accidentally swallowed the coin because he was talking too much! It stuck half-way down his throat. He started to choke. A doctor was called. Days passed. The coin stayed stuck. A weaker man might have panicked and choked to death. But Isambard had faced danger many times before. He put his engineer's mind to work. He designed a special table which could spin at high speed. He was strapped to the table, turned upside down and spun round. The force of the spin made the coin fly from his throat. Once again, Isambard's skill and calm had saved his life. He later wrote to a friend: 'At 4 1/2 (4.30), I was safely delivered of my little coin!'

There is no doubt that Isambard was very happy with his wife and children, and later, his grandchildren. But he admitted

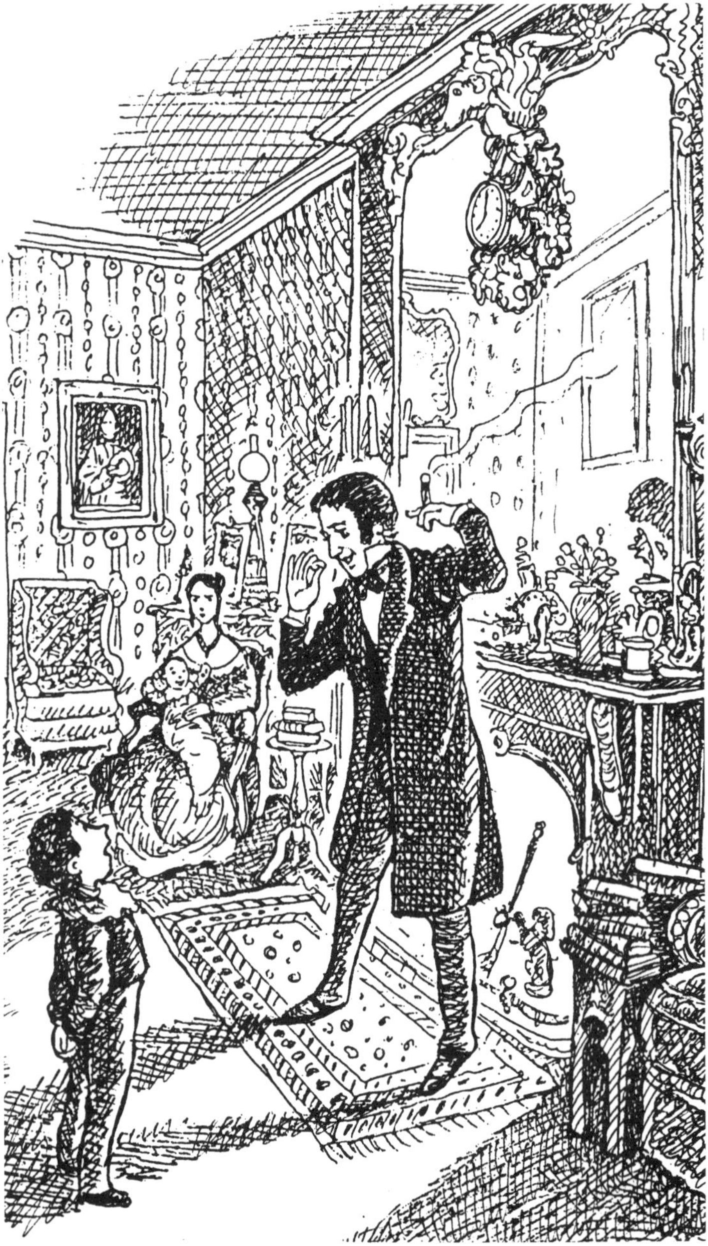

once in his diary: 'My profession is after all my only fit wife...'

Isambard could not have written a truer word. Right in the middle of an impressive railway career, which had already made him famous, he turned to a different area of engineering – ships.

Chapter Six
Three Ships

One day, in 1835, Isambard was at a meeting with the directors of the Great Western Railway Company. 'We're worried about this railway,' they told him. 'Will it ever make any money for us? Don't you think it's too long?'
Isambard didn't answer at first. He wasn't angry. He was thinking. Suddenly, he jumped to his feet and shouted: 'Why not make it longer, and have a steamboat to go from Bristol to New York, and call it the *Great Western?*'

Isambard's friends laughed and talked about something else. But he wasn't joking.

That night, he didn't go to bed at all. He wanted to think about his steamship.

There were already many steamships crossing the Atlantic Ocean to America. They had huge paddles to move the water. But the engines often broke down and they were not reliable for long journeys. All these steamships had one problem. They were not big enough to carry enough coal for the journey – they had to stop on the way to pick up more coal.

The next day, Isambard told a close friend, Thomas Guppy, 'I'm going to build a ship big enough to carry coal for a non-stop voyage from Bristol to New York.' His friend warned him that other companies were trying the same thing. 'Good!' replied Isambard, 'I like a race!'

A few months later, in 1836, Isambard and Thomas Guppy set up a company called the Great Western Steamship Company. Only one year later, he launched his steamship, the *Great Western*. It was larger than any other steamship, and carried 150 passengers, and 57 crew.

On 31 March, 1838, the great ship set off on her first voyage to America. It was a clear spring-like morning. As she sailed from the

Thames towards Bristol to pick up passengers, a terrible smell filled the air. Black smoke belched over the deck. There was a huge explosion in the boiler room where the steam was produced. Sea-water rushed in. The Captain of the ship climbed down the ladder to the boiler room to see what was wrong. Suddenly, something heavy hit him on the head and splashed into the water a long way below. He peered down. It was Isambard Kingdom Brunel, unconscious with his face in the water. The Captain called for ropes and they pulled poor Isambard out onto the deck. For the second time, he had been saved from a watery grave.

Many passengers were frightened. They refused to travel. The ship sailed with only seven passengers on board – and cows and cattle and chickens for the voyage. It crossed the Atlantic Ocean in only fifteen days, with coal to spare. Although its rival ship had arrived a day earlier, that ship had run out of coal and burned everything it could to make steam, including a passenger's doll!

The *Great Western* made sixty-seven Atlantic crossings after that. It was a very expensive ship to run. Isambard didn't make any profit from it. But although the *Great Western* had nearly killed its designer, it proved that such large steamships could make the long journey across the Atlantic Ocean.

Isambard could now have enjoyed his wealth and fame and spent more time with his family. But he was obsessed by the idea of building ships, just as his father had been by the Thames Tunnel so many years before.

Isambard Kingdom Brunel decided to build an even bigger steamship.

Five years later, early in the morning of 19 July, 1843, Prince Albert, the husband of Queen Victoria, boarded the Great Western Railway. He was travelling to Bristol. Next to him sat Isambard Kingdom Brunel. Prince Albert was going to launch Isambard's new ship, The *Great Britain*.

Nobody had ever built such an enormous ship before. And it was the first steamship to be made of iron. Instead of a paddle, there was a propeller. It was stronger and faster than any other ship. It carried 252 passengers and 130 crew.

It was a day of great celebration in Bristol. All the shops were closed. Flags were flying on the top of buildings. The riverside was

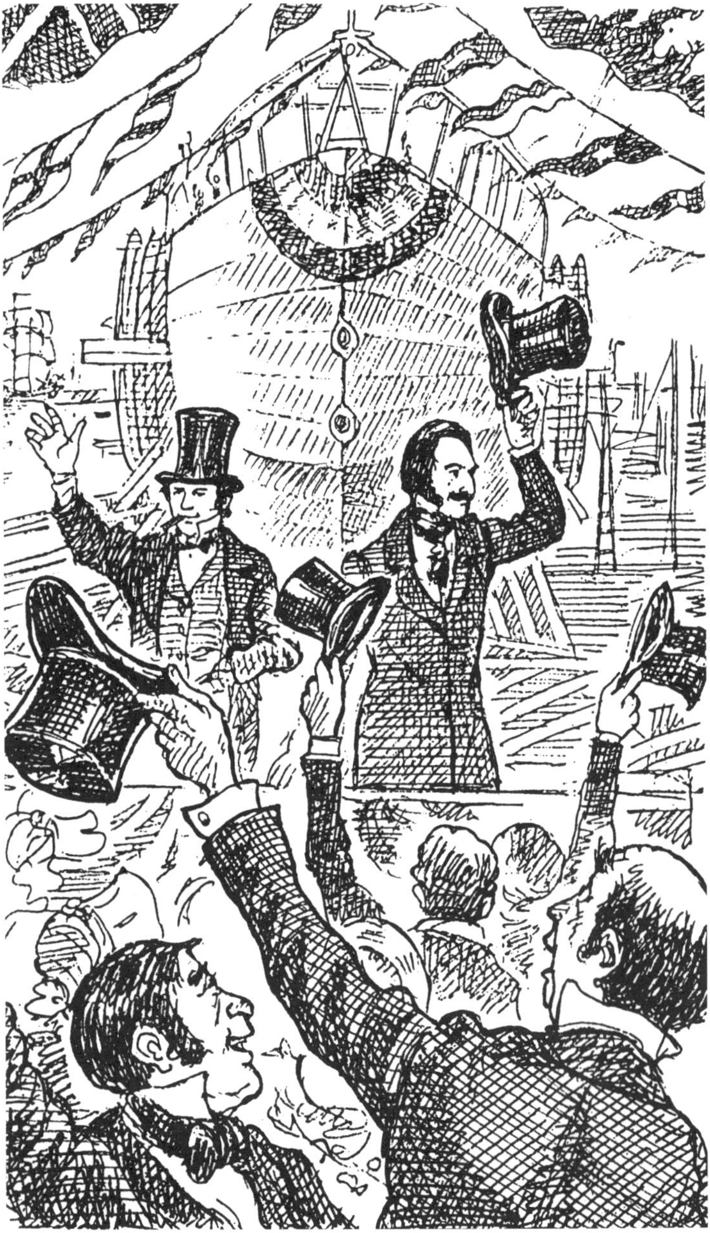

crowded with people. Isambard and the Prince went to a lunch for six hundred important people. Finally, the great moment came. As Prince Albert broke a bottle of champagne against the side of the ship, water rushed into the dry dock. The *Great Britain* floated into the River Avon to the sound of church bells and booming guns.

The *Great Britain's* first voyage was between Liverpool and New York in 1845. Unfortunately, a year later, she ran onto rocks on a beach in Ireland because the sea charts were wrongly drawn. Luckily, none of the one hundred and eighty passengers were hurt. And the ship was so strongly built that it didn't sink. Nobody knew how to pull the ship from the stormy seas. It was Isambard who sprang into action. He gave orders for a wooden wind-shield to be built to protect the ship from the winter weather. Then, in the spring, the *Great Britain* was pulled safely from the rocks. This ship went on to carry many passengers starting a new life in Australia. And, more importantly, Isambard's design was used a few years later for ships for the Royal Navy.

Isambard's head was always full of new

plans, new ideas and he couldn't just forget them. Although he was still building railways and re-designing a country house in Devon for his old age, he knew that he wanted to build an even bigger ship.

In 1851, Isambard was an important guest at the Great Exhibition. This was held at Crystal Palace in the middle of Hyde Park in London. It showed off Britain's great engineering skills. At this time, Britain was called 'the workshop of the world', and its railways and machinery were used in other countries.

Everybody wanted to shake Isambard's hand. A man who met him there wrote: 'Even to shake hands with one so remarkable was a thing to be remembered for a lifetime.'

The Great Exhibition fired Isambard's imagination again. He began to sketch a new ship. It would be called the *Great Eastern* and was to be the biggest ship ever built. It would carry four thousand passengers, an enormous number for that time. Isambard needed a partner to help him. He chose a man called John Scott Russell, an engineer. He and Isambard did not get on well. The ship was finished only after many arguments and years of worry, which lost money for the company.

The launch was constantly delayed. Finally, the great day came. Isambard did not think the launch would be easy. He didn't want anyone to watch in case it failed, although he did allow his son Henry to take a day off school to be with him. Unfortunately, the men running the company wanted to make some money out of the launch. They sold three thousand tickets so that people could watch. Isambard didn't know. Afterwards, he wrote: 'I learnt to my horror that all the world was invited…It was not right, it was cruel…'

Henry had never seen his father so angry. It was chaos in the shipyard. People swarmed all over the launch machinery. The ship slid a few yards towards the water, then stuck. Huge chains were brought to pull the ship into the water. They crashed on top of a man and killed him. The launch was cancelled.

Everyone was disappointed. People began to say that Isambard Kingdom Brunel had now taken too many chances. It was a crisis for Isambard. Was his public turning against him? For ten weeks, the ship refused to move. It rained and rained. On 31 January, the rain stopped at last. At six o'clock in the morning, when the sky was bright with stars, Isambard went to wake up Henry. 'It's time!' he told his sleepy son. At last, the *Great Eastern* floated sideways into the River Thames. During the last week, Isambard had gone without sleep for sixty hours. His company had run out of money.

This was the ship that slowly killed Isambard. He did not have enough strength to bounce back from these troubles. He was weak after all the years of hard work. His doctor told him to rest somewhere warm. Isambard went to Egypt with his family. He still had one ambition left - to sail on the *Great Eastern* – so he booked cabins for all his family for later that year. Isambard wrote very little in his diary now, except to say: 'I would not trouble you with an invalid's journal.'

Sadly, Isambard and his family never travelled on the great ship. Two days before the voyage, Isambard had his photograph taken beside the ship's funnels. He looked even smaller, bent and frail, and leaned on a stick. That was the last time he saw his ship. Minutes later, Isambard collapsed. He had

had a stroke and couldn't move. He was taken home and the ship sailed without him. He died a few days later, on 15 September, 1859. He was only fifty-three years old.

The *Great Eastern* was also used to carry thousands of people to Australia and America to start their new lives and she was used to lay a telegraph cable across the Atlantic Ocean. Now messages tapped in code could be sent between London and New York in only a few minutes. A letter took two or three weeks and there were no telephones yet.

Although this ship didn't make much money for the company, its design was also used for later ships, including battleships. Everyone said that it was a ship 'born out of her time.'

**** ✷ ****

Isambard Kingdom Brunel was a proud and ambitious man. He lived at a time when inventors and engineers were famous and could earn a lot of money – even if they did lose it again. They were like sportsmen or television entertainers today.

Isambard always had great plans. He

wanted to build bigger and better. He always looked for new challenges. And he *always* worked hard. He could go without sleep for weeks but he never lost his temper at work. Isambard's friends and colleagues were proud of him and understood his genius. He showed the way for other engineers.

Isambard lived up to his motto 'En Avant' which is the French for 'Forward' or 'Let's Go.' He was a man of action who knew great success and great failure. He was great because he could turn his mind to any engineering problem. In little more than thirty years, he designed and built tunnels, bridges, railways and ships.

How much Isambard Kingdom Brunel would have enjoyed our inventions today! Some of the children at the Great Exhibition in 1851 lived long enough to see the first motor car. If they had lived to be eighty years old, they might have seen one of the first aeroplanes.

I'm sure that if Isambard Kingdom Brunel had lived today, he would have built a space ship to go to the moon.

PLACES TO VISIT

BRISTOL

The Clifton Suspension Bridge

The Temple Meads Station

The SS *Great Britan* in the Bristol Docks

The City of Bristol Museum and Art Gallery
has portraits of Isambard and his wife

The University of Bristol
holds many Great Western Railway sketch books and other items

SALTASH

The Royal Albert Bridge
spans the River Tamar between Devon and Cornwall

LONDON

Paddington Station
A marble statue of Isambard Kingdom Brunel. The Great Western Hotel

The National Portrait Gallery
The British Museum and
The Science Museum
Sketch books, photos and paintings relating to I.K. Brunel

Brunel University Library
Engravings, drawings and photographs of Brunel's work

PORTSEA
(Portsmouth)
A plaque in Britain Street marks Brunel's birthplace

SWINDON
The Great Western Railway Museum

WILTSHIRE
The Box Tunnel
is on the Chippenham to Bath railway line

DEVON
Watcombe Park
I.K. Brunel's country house
The Trustees of Brunel Manor hold many Documents

IMPORTANT DATES

1806
Isambard Kingdom Brunel born

1820
Isambard goes to France

1822
Isambard returns from France

1825
Work begins on the Thames Tunnel

1828
Work stops on the Thames Tunnel

1829
Isambard enters Clifton Bridge competition

1830
Isambard enters second competition

1831
Work begins on the Clifton Bridge
Work stops in October after the Bristol riots

1833
Survey for the Great Western Railway

1834
Work begins again on the Thames Tunnel

1835
Work begins again on the Clifton Bridge
Great Western Steamship Company formed

1836
Marriage to Mary Horsley
Work begins on the *Great Western*

1837
Great Western launched

1838
Isambard the Third born
Great Western's first voyage
Design begun for the *Great Britain*

1839
Work begins on the *Great Britain*

1841
Opening of the whole railway line
London-Bristol

1842
Henry Marc born

1843
Opening of the Thames Tunnel
The *Great Britain* launched

1845
The *Great Britain's* first voyage

1846
Mary born

1848
Work begins on the Saltash Bridge

1852
Designs begun for the *Great Eastern*

1853
Work begins on the *Great Eastern*

1858
Launch of the *Great Eastern*
Isambard goes to Egypt to rest

1859
Royal Albert Bridge at Saltash completed
The *Great Eastern's* first voyage
Isambard dies on 15 September

1864
The Bristol Suspension Bridge is completed